Printed in China

ISBN: 978-1-926884-05-9

 ISBN: 978-1-926884-05-9

Contents
Grade 3

ISBN: 978-1-926884-05-9

ISBN: 978-1-926884-05-9

Story 1

The Monkey's Heart

Characters

a monkey

a crocodile husband

a crocodile wife

ISBN: 978-1-926884-05-9

1

Once there was a wise monkey. He lived in a forest near a wide river.

In that same river lived two huge and mean crocodiles. They were husband and wife.

1. **Where did the monkey live?**
2. **What did the crocodiles want to have for dinner?**

ISBN: 978-1-926884-05-9

One day, the crocodiles saw the monkey sitting on the branch of a tree.

Point to

the synonym of "large"

ISBN: 978-1-926884-05-9

The crocodile husband thought up a plan to eat the monkey's heart.

1

He waited until the monkey came down from the tree to drink from the river.

1. **Why did the monkey come down from the tree?**
2. **Why couldn't the monkey get to the other side of the river?**

ISBN: 978-1-926884-05-9

"Monkey, why do you live on this side of the river?" asked the crocodile. "The fruit on the other side is much larger and sweeter".

Say

the two words that rhyme with "cried"

ISBN: 978-1-926884-05-9

1

The monkey was delighted and accepted the crocodile's offer. He climbed onto the crocodile's back to cross the river.

1. **How did the monkey cross the river?**

2. **Why did the crocodile dive underwater?**

ISBN: 978-1-926884-05-9

Suddenly, the crocodile dived underwater. The monkey **struggled** in the water, **gasping** for breath.

"You should never trust a crocodile. I'll drown you and eat your heart for dinner with my wife," said the crocodile with an evil smile.

New WORDS

struggled **gasping**

ISBN: 978-1-926884-05-9

The monkey was in **trouble**.

Then he pointed to the figs on the trees.

"We monkeys don't keep our hearts in our bodies; we hang them on trees."

1 **What did the monkey point to?**

2 **What did the monkey agree to do?**

ISBN: 978-1-926884-05-9

The crocodile believed what the monkey said.

The monkey agreed, and the crocodile carried him back to shore.

New WORDS

trouble **spare**

ISBN: 978-1-926884-05-9

Once they neared shore, the monkey jumped off the crocodile's back and climbed up a fig tree. He laughed at the crocodile and playfully ate a fig.

1

1 **What did the monkey playfully eat?**

2 **How did the monkey describe the crocodile?**

ISBN: 978-1-926884-05-9

"You might be large and powerful, but you aren't very smart," the monkey shouted.

Point to

the antonym of "weak"

ISBN: 978-1-926884-05-9

1

1 Can monkeys live without their hearts in their bodies?

2 How did the crocodile husband feel?

ISBN: 978-1-926884-05-9

The crocodile husband felt very foolish. He never tried to trick the monkey again.

Say

the word that rhymes with "smart"

ISBN: 978-1-926884-05-9

Do You Remember?

Look at the picture clues and fill in the blanks to complete the sentences. Then put the events in order from 1 to 4.

☐ Once they reached the shore, the monkey jumped off and climbed up a ______________ .

☐ The monkey told the crocodile that monkeys hung their ______________ on trees.

☐ The monkey climbed onto the crocodile's back to cross the ______________ .

☐ The ______________ tried to drown the monkey.

 ISBN: 978-1-926884-05-9

Story 1

Missing Words

Fill in the blanks to complete the paragraph.

climbed **shore** **fig** **plan**

smart **crocodile** **monkey**

The monkey was 1._______________ . He came up with a 2._______________ to trick the crocodile. When they reached the 3._______________ , the 4._______________ jumped off the crocodile's back and 5._______________ up a fig tree. He laughed at the 6._______________ and then playfully ate a 7._______________ .

ISBN: 978-1-926884-05-9

Story 1

Fun with Phonics

Say what each bubble is pointing to. Write the consonant blend of each word.

pl sn br cr fr tr

 ISBN: 978-1-926884-05-9

Sentence Smart

The verb is missing in each sentence. Rewrite the sentence by adding the verb in the correct place.

1. The monkey in the water.

2.

The monkey to the figs on the trees.

3. The monkey at the crocodile.

1. ______________________________

2. ______________________________

3. ______________________________

ISBN: 978-1-926884-05-9

Describe Them!

Draw lines to match the adjectives with the pictures. Then complete the sentences with the adjectives to describe the crocodile.

mean •

wide •

foolish •

wise •

huge •

sweet •

powerful •

I feel ______________ .

The ____________ and ____________ crocodile is ____________ but not very smart.

ISBN: 978-1-926884-05-9

Story 2

The Donkey's Journey

Characters

ISBN: 978-1-926884-05-9

Once there was a man. He lived with his son on a small farm. He owned a donkey. One day, his donkey had a little foal.

2

1 **How many donkeys did the man want to keep?**

2 **Where would the man sell the young donkey?**

ISBN: 978-1-926884-05-9

The man was troubled. He did not need two donkeys, so he decided to sell the young donkey at the market.

Say

the word that means "young donkey"

ISBN: 978-1-926884-05-9

The market was far away and it would be a long trip.

The man did not want to make the young donkey tired, so he and his son carried the donkey on a pole.

2

1 **How did the man and his son take the donkey to the market?**

2 **Why did the villagers laugh at the man and his son?**

ISBN: 978-1-926884-05-9

When they reached a village, the villagers pointed and laughed at them.

Point to

the villager who is selling fruit

ISBN: 978-1-926884-05-9

So the man let his son ride on the donkey.

1 **Did the man agree with what the villagers said?**

2 **Why did the woman scold the man's son?**

 ISBN: 978-1-926884-05-9

When they reached the next village, they met an old woman.

"You're a **selfish** boy," the woman **scolded** the son. "Your father is older than you. You should let him ride the donkey."

New WORDS

selfish scolded

The son agreed with what the old woman said, too. He jumped off the donkey and let his father ride on it instead.

They continued their journey to the market.

1 Did the son do what the old woman said?

2 Where did the man and his son come by the girl?

ISBN: 978-1-926884-05-9

Soon after, they came by a girl who was fetching water from a well.

"Your son is young. He should be riding the donkey, not you!" said the girl angrily.

Point to

the antonym of "old"

ISBN: 978-1-926884-05-9

The man came up with an idea. "Climb up here, son. Let's ride the donkey together," he said.

1. **Who suggested riding the donkey together?**

2. **Why did the farmer shout at the man and his son?**

ISBN: 978-1-926884-05-9

When they came to a field, a farmer saw them riding the donkey and shouted at them.

Say

the word that rhymes with "healed"

ISBN: 978-1-926884-05-9

At last, the man and his son decided to lead the donkey by a rope and walk to the market.

There, they sold the donkey to a nice family. They were happy and relieved.

1 **How did they get the donkey to the market at last?**

2 **Who bought the donkey?**

ISBN: 978-1-926884-05-9

On their way home, they talked about their journey to the market.

New WORDS

impossible please

Story 2

Do You Remember?

Write the letters to match the people with what they said.

A Your son is young. He should be riding the donkey, not you!

B Your father is older than you. You should let him ride the donkey.

C That donkey is too young to carry both of you.

D People are not meant to carry donkeys!

ISBN: 978-1-926884-05-9

Story 2

Missing Words

Fill in the blanks to complete the story.

The Donkey's Journey

A man wanted to sell his young donkey at the 1. ____________ (market/fair). At first, he and his son carried the donkey on a 2. ____________ (wagon/pole). Then they took turns 3. ____________ (carrying/riding) the donkey. After that, they 4. ____________ (rode/left) the donkey together. At last, they decided to lead the donkey by a 5. ____________ (chain/rope). When they reached the market, they 6. ____________ (sold/gave) the donkey to a nice family.

ISBN: 978-1-926884-05-9

Story 2

Fun with Phonics

Say the words. Find and circle their homophones in the word search. Then write them on the lines.

Homophones are words that sound the same. The words in the word search are all from the story.

Homophones

knead	______	sew	______
write	______	won	______
knot	______	wood	______
cell	______	too	______

w	o	u	l	d	e	f	j	l	s	d	h	k
e	b	d	s	r	i	t	m	b	e	m	o	j
h	r	i	g	h	t	w	f	i	l	p	n	e
z	l	u	w	j	p	o	t	n	l	c	e	d
n	e	e	d	v	s	d	x	q	s	n	o	t
b	i	c	m	g	o	n	b	r	y	c	l	e

ISBN: 978-1-926884-05-9

Sentence Smart

Complete the sentences with the words in the pictures.

1. The donkey had ______________________________ .

2. They carried the donkey ______________________ .

3. They met a girl _____________________________ .

4. They ______________________________ together.

ISBN: 978-1-926884-05-9

Story 2

My Donkey's Journey

Imagine that you and your friend are getting a donkey to the market. Check and describe how you would do so. Then check the reasons for your choice.

Ways to Get a Donkey to the Market

carry ○

one rides ○

lead ○

both ride ○

The Way You Choose...

____

____

Reasons:

- ○ saving our energy
- ○ showing our care for the donkey
- ○ giving the donkey some exercise
- ○ saving the donkey's energy
- ○ keeping ourselves fit
- ✔ _______________________________

____

ISBN: 978-1-926884-05-9

Story 3

An Adventure by the Sea

Characters

Carl

Ted and Jane

pirates

ISBN: 978-1-926884-05-9

3

One sunny day, Ted, Jane, and Carl went to the beach.

1 **What did the children use to decorate the sandcastle?**

2 **Why did Jane cry?**

ISBN: 978-1-926884-05-9

They built a huge **sandcastle**. Jane **decorated** it with seashells. Ted put a flag on top.

The children bought ice cream, but a seagull snatched Jane's away.

New WORDS

sandcastle	decorated

ISBN: 978-1-926884-05-9

They caught little crabs. While Carl was trying to catch a green crab, it nipped his finger.

3

1 **What did the crab do to Carl?**

2 **What was Jane counting?**

ISBN: 978-1-926884-05-9

Then Ted and Carl splashed in the water.
Jane caught shrimps with her net.

Say

the synonym of "bit"

ISBN: 978-1-926884-05-9

Suddenly, huge rain clouds covered the sun. The sea and sky turned grey and rain poured down.

The children ran to take shelter in a cave.

3

1. **Why did the children run to the cave?**

2. **What was glittering in the cave?**

ISBN: 978-1-926884-05-9

Deep in the cave, they saw something **glittering** in the corner. It was a chest filled with **treasure**!

New WORDS

glittering | treasure

ISBN: 978-1-926884-05-9

Then they heard voices and were shocked to find that they were surrounded by fierce pirates. They had nowhere to hide!

3

1 **Whose voices did the children hear?**

2 **Why were the children frightened?**

ISBN: 978-1-926884-05-9

Suddenly, bright lights lit the entire cave. The children froze with fear. They did not know what to do.

Say

the word that rhymes with "quite"

ISBN: 978-1-926884-05-9

3

1 **What were the "pirates" doing?**

2 **What was the unusual and exciting experience?**

ISBN: 978-1-926884-05-9

The director let the children stay and watch. It was a truly unusual and exciting experience that they would never forget.

Point to

the director of the movie

ISBN: 978-1-926884-05-9

When the filming was over, one of the pirates gave the children some "treasure".

Jane got a pretty necklace. She put it on at once.

3

1 **Did Jane like the necklace?**

2 **What did the children see in the sky?**

ISBN: 978-1-926884-05-9

The children left the cave.

The rain had stopped. It was sunny again, with a beautiful rainbow across the clear blue sky.

Say

the two words that are synonyms

ISBN: 978-1-926884-05-9

Do You Remember?

Fill in the blanks with the words that the people say. Then put the events in order from 1 to 5.

An Adventure by the Sea

Events in Order

☐ The pirates told them that they were actually filming a ______________ .

☐ The children found a treasure chest and were suddenly surrounded by ______________ .

☐ The children built a ______________ on the beach.

☐ Suddenly, it rained and the children took shelter in a ______________ .

☐ When the filming was over, the children were given some ______________ .

 ISBN: 978-1-926884-05-9

Missing Words

Name the things mentioned in the story. Then complete the sentences with the words you have written.

Things Mentioned

1. ____________________
2. ____________________
3. ____________________
4. ____________________
5. ____________________

An Adventure by the Sea

In a ____________ by the ____________ , the children found a ____________ filled with ____________ . They also met some people filming a movie about ____________ .

ISBN: 978-1-926884-05-9

Fun with Phonics

Unscramble the letters and write the words. Then say the words and write the ones with long vowels in the box.

1. ______________ artepi

2. ______________ locud

3. ______________ bwoiran

4. ______________ sepda

5. ______________ dasncsalte

6. ______________ laip

7. ______________ rabc

8. ______________ sseellah

Words with Long Vowels

ISBN: 978-1-926884-05-9

Sentence Smart

Add the given adjective in the correct place in each sentence. Rewrite the sentence on the lines.

1. A crab nipped Carl's finger. (green)
2. Rain clouds covered the sun. (huge)
3. The actors looked like pirates. (real)
4. Jane got a necklace from a pirate. (pretty)

ISBN: 978-1-926884-05-9

Story 3

Join the Words!

Use the words in the pictures to form compound words.

Compound Words

1. ______________ + ______________ = ______________________

2. ______________ + ______________ = ______________________

3. ______________ + ______________ = ______________________

4. ______________ + ______________ = ______________________

5. ______________ + ______________ = ______________________

6. ______________ + ______________ = ______________________

ISBN: 978-1-926884-05-9

Story 4

The Money Bag

Characters

a husband

a wife

a giant

ISBN: 978-1-926884-05-9

4

Once there was a poor **couple**. They lived in a little hut near a forest, where they went to cut wood every day.

1. **Why did the couple go to the forest?**

2. **Where would the husband sell the bundle of wood?**

ISBN: 978-1-926884-05-9

One day, the husband left a **bundle** of wood outside the hut and decided to sell it at the market the following day.

New WORDS

couple	bundle

ISBN: 978-1-926884-05-9

4

The next morning, they were astonished to find that the bundle of wood was gone.

1 **Why did the husband hide in the bundle of wood?**

2 **What happened while he was sleeping?**

ISBN: 978-1-926884-05-9

The husband was angry. He came up with a plan to catch the thief. That night, he hid in a bundle of wood and waited.

But he fell asleep while he was waiting and did not notice it when the bundle rose slowly into the sky.

Point to

the antonym of "happy"

4

When the husband woke up and found that he was in the sky, with a giant in front of him, he was **terrified**.

1 **What terrified the husband?**

2 **Why did the giant help the man?**

ISBN: 978-1-926884-05-9

The giant told the husband that he wanted to help him because the poor man was honest and hard-working. He gave him a money bag.

New WORD

terrified

ISBN: 978-1-926884-05-9

When the poor man got back home, he did as he was told. He took one coin from the bag every day. They used the coins to buy food and saved the rest.

4

1 **What did the couple use the coins for?**

2 **Why did the husband need more coins?**

 ISBN: 978-1-926884-05-9

"We've saved enough money to buy an ox!" said the wife happily.

But the husband wanted a large house. He ignored what the giant had told him and took many coins from the bag.

Say

the word that describes the house

ISBN: 978-1-926884-05-9

1 What happened when the house was built?

2 Why were the couple shocked the next morning?

 ISBN: 978-1-926884-05-9

Worse yet, the next morning, the couple woke up to find themselves in their old, **shabby** hut.

New WORDS

worse   shabby

ISBN: 978-1-926884-05-9

4

The husband realized that he should not have been so greedy. He cut wood in the forest like before.

1 What did the husband realize?

2 Were the couple happy in the end?

ISBN: 978-1-926884-05-9

From then on, the man lived a simple and honest life with his wife.

Point to

the antonym of "after"

ISBN: 978-1-926884-05-9

Do You Remember?

Answer the questions with the help of the pictures.

1. Who lived in a little hut?
2. Where did the couple go to cut wood?
3. What did the husband leave outside the hut one day?
4. What did the giant give the husband?

The Money Bag

1. ____________________ lived in a little hut.
2. The couple went to ____________________ to cut wood.
3. The husband left ____________________ outside the hut one day.
4. The giant gave the husband ____________________ .

 ISBN: 978-1-926884-05-9

Story 4

Missing Words

Fill in the missing words with the code given.

The husband and his ________ (23 9 6 5) took a ________ (7 15 12 4) coin from the ________ (13 15 14 5 25) bag every day.

However, the husband became ________ (7 18 5 5 4 25). He took many coins from the bag to ________ (2 21 9 12 4) a large house. Then no more coins would ________ (6 1 12 12) out of the bag and the large house turned back into a ________ (19 8 1 2 2 25) hut.

Code

A = 1	B = 2	C = 3
D = 4	E = 5	F = 6
G = 7	H = 8	I = 9
J = 10	K = 11	L = 12
M = 13	N = 14	O = 15
P = 16	Q = 17	R = 18
S = 19	T = 20	U = 21
V = 22	W = 23	X = 24
Y = 25	Z = 26	

ISBN: 978-1-926884-05-9

Story 4

Fun with Phonics

Say what each bubble is pointing to. Write the vowel diphthong of each word. Then list the vowel diphthongs and give an example.

Vowel Diphthongs

- ________
- ________
- ________
- ________
- oy (my example: __________)

These vowel diphthongs contain the letter "o". There is one more vowel diphthong - "oy". Give an example of a word with this diphthong.

ISBN: 978-1-926884-05-9

Story 4

Sentence Smart

Write what the man and his wife say in the speech bubbles.

"When we've saved enough money," said the wife, "we can buy an ox."	*"I want a large house," said the man, "but I need more coins."*

ISBN: 978-1-926884-05-9

The Gift from the Giant

If you were the giant, what would you give to the husband as a gift and why? Draw the gift in the box and write the reason.

Reason for giving this gift:

____

____

____

ISBN: 978-1-926884-05-9

Story 5

Sally's Day at the Theme Park

Characters

Mom and Dad

Sally

a princess

ISBN: 978-1-926884-05-9

Sally went to the theme park with her parents. She was excited, but her parents only had enough money for her to go on one ride.

5

1 **Why couldn't Sally go on all the rides she liked?**

2 **What were the children on the Mermaid Ride doing?**

ISBN: 978-1-926884-05-9

She looked at the children laughing and **screaming** as they **splashed** into the water on the Mermaid Ride.

New WORDS

screaming	splashed

ISBN: 978-1-926884-05-9

5

The Big Dipper looked exciting and the carousel turned fast.

1. **Where were the horses?**
2. **What was in the tunnel?**

ISBN: 978-1-926884-05-9

At last, Sally chose the Ghost Train. She wanted to try the eerie ride.

The train went into a dark tunnel. There were ghosts, monsters, and bats. It was fun and scary!

Point to

the antonym of "boring"

ISBN: 978-1-926884-05-9

5

1. Where did Sally and her parents have tea?

2. What happened when it was time to go home?

ISBN: 978-1-926884-05-9

Sally sat by the Princess's Castle. She did not know what to do. Above her was a picture of the princess.

Say

the word that rhymes with "key"

ISBN: 978-1-926884-05-9

5

Suddenly, the princess in the picture moved. She went to Sally and smiled.

"Hello, Sally!" said the princess. "Today you went on just one ride. Do you want to try more?"

1 Where did the princess come from?

2 Who rode on the Big Dipper with Sally?

ISBN: 978-1-926884-05-9

The mermaid took Sally on the Mermaid Ride.

Captain Fearless took Sally up and down the Big Dipper. It was exciting.

Say

the words with three syllables

ISBN: 978-1-926884-05-9

5

She rode a white horse on the carousel.

She spun round and round with the princess and the fairies on the Fairy Swings.

1. **Did the princess go on the carousel with Sally?**

2. **What did they do in the Princess's Castle?**

ISBN: 978-1-926884-05-9

Then they all had tea in the Princess's Castle. After all the fun and **excitement**, Sally was tired. She dozed off.

New WORD

excitement

ISBN: 978-1-926884-05-9

5

"Wake up, Sally! It's time to go home," came the voice of her dad.

Sally woke up and found herself in the café, with her parents beside her.

1. **Where was Sally when she woke up?**
2. **Do you think that all the fun Sally had was real?**

ISBN: 978-1-926884-05-9

Then she saw the princess in the picture wink at her.

"Wow, it was real!" thought Sally happily.

show

how to wink

Do You Remember?

Name the rides that Sally went on before and after she met the princess.

Before Meeting the Princess:

____

After Meeting the Princess:

____

____

____

____

ISBN: 978-1-926884-05-9

Missing Words

Fill in the blanks with the antonyms of the given words.

Antonyms of these words

1. rainy
2. few
3. first
4. bright
5. lovely
6. before
7. bad

One 1. ____________ day, Sally went to the theme park with her parents. She liked 2. ____________ of the rides, but she could only choose one ride to go on. At 3. ____________ , she chose the Ghost Train. The train went into a 4. ____________ tunnel, where they saw 5. ____________ bats, ghosts, and monsters. 6. ____________ the ride, Sally and her parents had tea in the café. They had a 7. ____________ time at the theme park.

Fun with Phonics

Complete each word with the correct three-letter consonant blend. Then fill in the blanks with the words and read the sentences aloud.

Three-letter Consonant Blends

- scr
- spl
- spr
- str

1. _____awberries
2. _____abble
3. _____eamed
4. _____ashed
5. _____ong
6. _____ingtime

7. Captain Fearless looks ______________ and powerful!

8. It was ______________ when Sally went to the theme park with her parents.

9. Sally and her parents ate ______________ and had tea in the café.

10. Sally played "______________" with the princess and the fairies in the Princess's Castle.

11. The children ______________ as they ______________ into the water on the Mermaid Ride.

ISBN: 978-1-926884-05-9

Sentence Smart

Rewrite the sentences with the correct capitalization and punctuation.

1. are you having fun: sally!
2. wow? this is exciting. mermaid,
3. "sally; it is time to go home," dad said.
4. "was that just a dream or was it real, thought sally!

1. ______________________________

____

2. ______________________________

____

3. ______________________________

____

4. ______________________________

____

ISBN: 978-1-926884-05-9

Describe Them!

Draw lines to show which characters took Sally on the rides. Then write a sentence to describe each character.

About the Characters:

- ____
- ____
- ____
- ____

ISBN: 978-1-926884-05-9

Story 6

Diamonds and Toads

Characters

a young girl

a mother and a sister

an old woman

ISBN: 978-1-926884-05-9

6

Once there was a young girl. She lived with her mother and her elder sister. Her sister was her mother's favourite. They were both lazy and always picky.

1. **Which daughter was the mother's favourite?**

2. **Was the mother kind and hard-working?**

ISBN: 978-1-926884-05-9

The young girl, on the other hand, was kind and hard-working. She was not like her mother or sister at all.

Say

the two words that are antonyms

Every day, the young girl walked a long way to **fetch** water from a well.

One day, there was an old woman sitting by the well. "I'm thirsty. Will you please give me a drink of water?" asked the old woman.

6

The girl filled her jug with water and gave it to the woman.

1 **Was the well near the girl's home?**

2 **What did the old woman ask for?**

ISBN: 978-1-926884-05-9

The woman was **actually** a good fairy. She waved her arms and said, "You're a gentle and caring girl. I'll give you a gift for being so kind."

As the girl thanked her, a rose and two pearls fell out of her mouth.

New WORDS

fetch	actually

6

The girl did not know what to do. She quickly ran home to tell her mother and sister what had happened.

As she spoke, diamonds and pearls dropped from her mouth and rolled on the floor.

1 **What fell out of the girl's mouth as she spoke?**

2 **What did the mother tell her older daughter to do?**

ISBN: 978-1-926884-05-9

The mother was greedy. She wanted to get more from the fairy.

So the next day, the older daughter went to the well.

Say

the word that rhymes with "sweetie"

6

She saw a rich woman sitting by the well. The woman asked the girl for a drink of water.

"She's not the fairy I'm looking for," thought the girl.

1 **Was the rich woman really the fairy?**

2 **Did the elder sister get the same gift as her sister?**

 ISBN: 978-1-926884-05-9

Suddenly, the rich woman turned into the fairy.

"You're such a rude and **selfish** girl. I'll give you a gift, but yours will be very different from your sister's," said the woman.

The girl was scared. She ran home at once.

New WORDS

suddenly **selfish**

When the girl arrived home, she tried to tell her mother what had happened, but toads and snakes filled her mouth.

6

1. **What "gift" did the older daughter get from the fairy?**

2. **Why did the younger daughter leave?**

ISBN: 978-1-926884-05-9

The mother was furious. She blamed everything on her younger daughter.

The young girl left sadly.

a furious face

ISBN: 978-1-926884-05-9

6

The girl wept as she walked along the path and left a trail of jewels behind her.

A prince travelling on the same path saw the jewels. He followed the trail all the way to the girl.

1. How did the prince find the girl?

2. What happened to the girl in the end?

ISBN: 978-1-926884-05-9

When they met, the prince saw that the girl was gentle and kind, and the girl knew that the prince was a just and noble young man.

They fell in love and were happily married.

Point to

the past tense form of "weep"

Story 6

Do You Remember?

Fill in the blanks to complete the sentences. Then write the letters to put the events in order.

A The girls' ____________ was angry and told the young girl to leave.

B Her sister did not help the fairy. As a punishment, ____________ and snakes fell from her mouth.

C Once there was a hard-working young girl who had a lazy mother and ____________ .

D After the young girl helped a fairy, diamonds, roses, and ____________ dropped from her mouth.

Diamonds and Toads

Events in Order:

____ , ____ , ____ , ____

ISBN: 978-1-926884-05-9

Missing Words

Unscramble the letters and write the words on the lines to describe the characters.

The Characters in the Story

1. You're ________ (ured) and ________ (heslisf)!

2. The young girl was ________ (ainrcg), ________ (egnetl), kind, and ________ (darh-roinkwg).

3. The ________ (deeryg) mother became ________ (foiuurs) and told the girl to leave.

4. A ________ (ujst) and ________ (lnboe) prince met the girl and they fell in love.

ISBN: 978-1-926884-05-9

Story 6

Fun with Phonics

Circle the words from the story that contain double consonants. Then put the words in the correct boxes and read them aloud.

Diamonds and Toads

The sister arrived at the well and saw a rich woman sitting there. The woman asked her for a drink of water but the sister refused. Suddenly, the woman's appearance changed. She was actually the fairy! She wanted to teach the girl a lesson, so she gave her a very different gift from her younger sister's – toads and snakes fell from the elder sister's mouth as she spoke!

Double Consonants

dd

ff

ll

pp

rr

ss

tt

ISBN: 978-1-926884-05-9

Story 6

Sentence Smart

Put the words in order and write the sentences. Then write the letters to match the sentences with the correct pictures.

1. always they angry were .

   ______________________________ [ ]

2. woman a the was fairy .

   ______________________________ [ ]

3. the was rich thirsty woman .

   ______________________________ [ ]

4. jewels prince the the saw .

   ______________________________ [ ]

ISBN: 978-1-926884-05-9

Story 6

What Happened Next?

The mother went to the well to meet the fairy herself. The fairy changed herself into the young girl. Write what the mother said to the fairy.

Next...

Draw what she got from the fairy.

ISBN: 978-1-926884-05-9

My Creative Stories

Complete the stories in your own words. Then cut along the red lines and staple the pages in order.

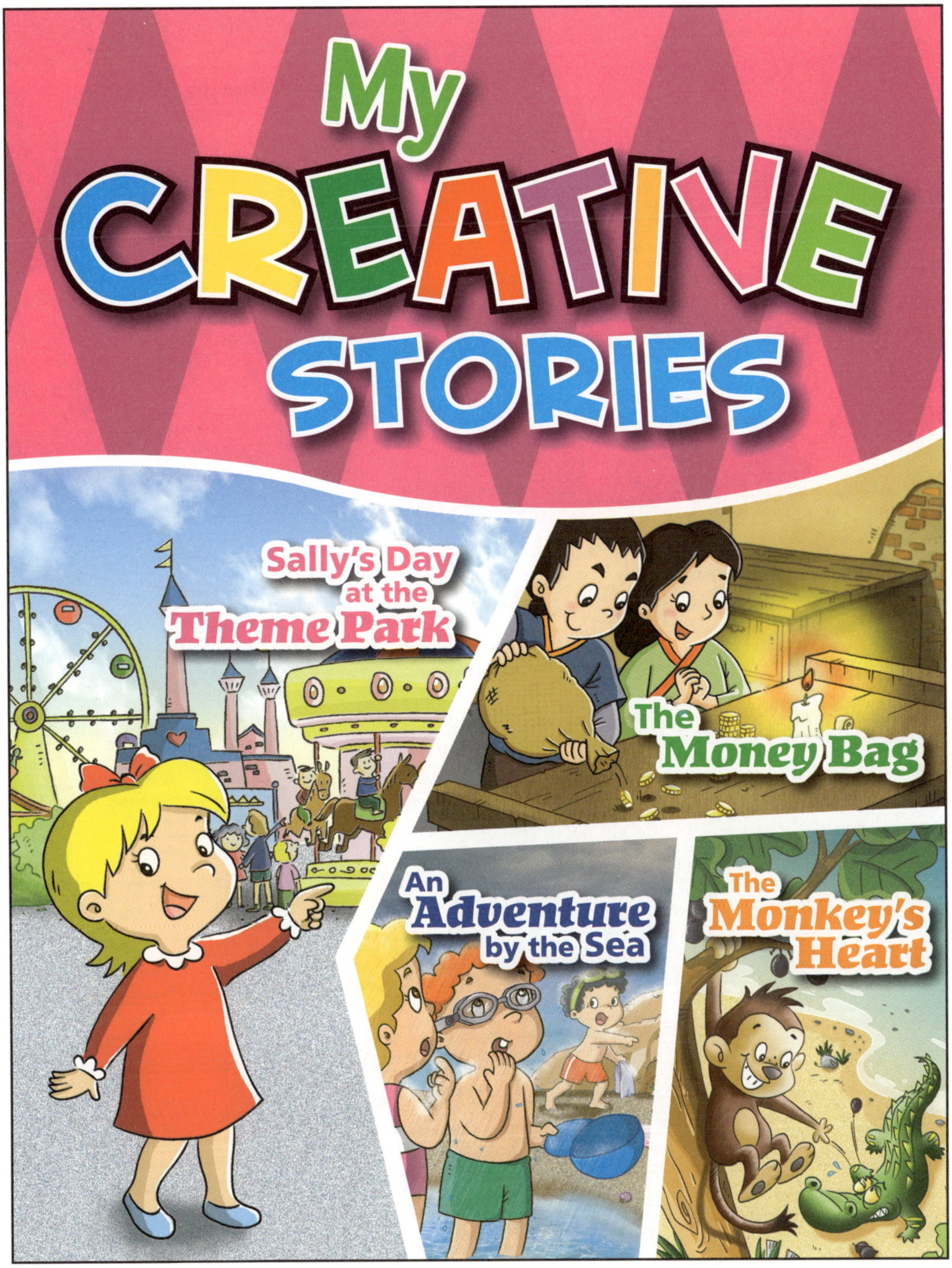

ISBN: 978-1-926884-05-9

ISBN: 978-1-926884-05-9

3

ISBN: 978-1-926884-05-9

 ISBN: 978-1-926884-05-9

ISBN: 978-1-926884-05-9

6

ISBN: 978-1-926884-05-9

Then the children ______________
____
Suddenly, they saw bright lights.
The pirates in the cave were making a movie.
It's cool.
When the filming was over, one of the pirates gave the children some treasure.
7

Tell your friend the story of *The Monkey's Heart* with the help of this page.

8

ISBN: 978-1-926884-05-9

A Paper Monkey

Fold and then cut along the dotted lines to make a paper monkey.

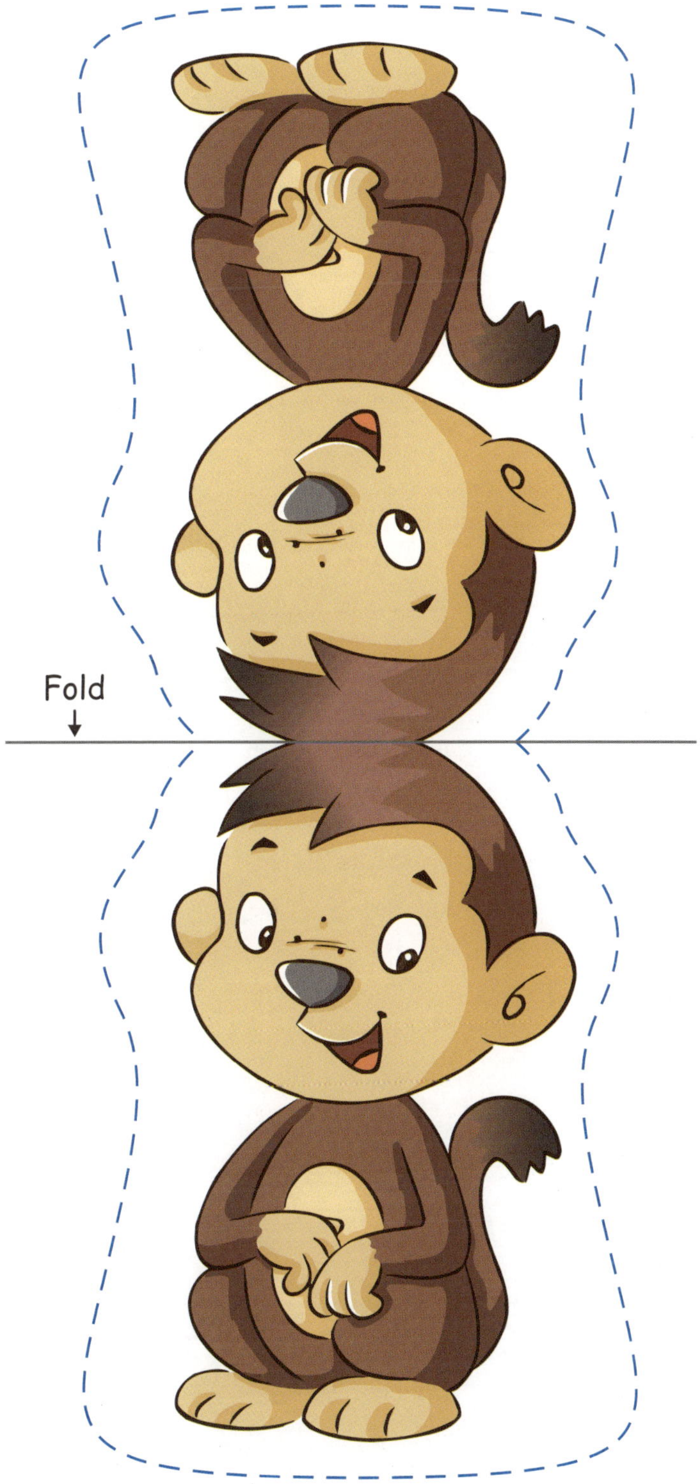

You can use this paper monkey and the paper crocodile on page 123 when you tell your friend my story.

ISBN: 978-1-926884-05-9

A Paper Crocodile

Fold and then cut along the dotted lines to make a paper crocodile.

ISBN: 978-1-926884-05-9

ISBN: 978-1-926884-05-9

Answers

Story 1
The Monkey's Heart

p. 18 Do You Remember?

4 ; tree
3 ; hearts
1 ; river
2 ; crocodile

p. 19 Missing Words

1. smart
2. plan
3. shore
4. monkey
5. climbed
6. crocodile
7. fig

p. 20 Fun with Phonics

fruit ; branch ; trunk ; plant ; crocodile ; snout

p. 21 Sentence Smart

1. The monkey struggled in the water.
2. The monkey pointed to the figs on the trees.
3. The monkey laughed at the crocodile.

p. 22 Describe Them!

foolish
(Suggested answers)
huge ; mean ; powerful

Story 2
The Donkey's Journey

p. 36 Do You Remember?

farmer: C
girl: A
old woman: B
villager: D

p. 37 Missing Words

1. market
2. pole
3. riding
4. rode
5. rope
6. sold

ISBN: 978-1-926884-05-9

p. 38 Fun with Phonics

need ; so
right ; one
not ; would
sell ; two

w	o	u	l	d	e	f	j	l	s	d	h	k
e	b	d	s	r	i	t	m	b	e	m	o	j
h	r	i	g	h	t	w	f	i	l	p	n	o
z	l	u	w	j	p	o	t	n	l	c	e	d
n	e	e	d	v	s	d	x	q	s	n	o	t
b	i	c	m	g	o	n	b	r	y	c	l	e

p. 39 Sentence Smart

1. a little foal
2. on a pole
3. by a well
4. rode the donkey

p. 40 My Donkey's Journey

(Individual answers)

Story 3
An Adventure by the Sea

p. 54 Do You Remember?

4 ; movie
3 ; pirates
1 ; sandcastle
2 ; cave
5 ; treasure

p. 55 Missing Words

1. beach
2. cave
3. pirates
4. treasure
5. chest

cave ; beach ; chest ; treasure ; pirates

p. 56 Fun with Phonics

1. pirate
2. cloud
3. rainbow
4. spade
5. sandcastle
6. pail
7. crab
8. seashell

Words with Long Vowels:
pirate ; rainbow ; spade ; pail ; seashell

p. 57 Sentence Smart

1. A green crab nipped Carl's finger.
2. Huge rain clouds covered the sun.
3. The actors looked like real pirates.
4. Jane got a pretty necklace from a pirate.

ISBN: 978-1-926884-05-9

p. 58 Join the Words!

1. sand ; castle ; sandcastle
2. rain ; bow ; rainbow
3. sea ; shell ; seashell
4. jelly ; fish ; jellyfish
5. neck ; lace ; necklace
6. sun ; glasses ; sunglasses

Story 4
The Money Bag

p. 72 Do You Remember?

1. A couple
2. the forest
3. a bundle of wood
4. a money bag

p. 73 Missing Words

wife ; gold ; money ; greedy ; build ; fall ; shabby

p. 74 Fun with Phonics

bough ; brow ; coin ; roof ; mouth ; flower

oi

oo

ou

ow

(Individual example)

p. 75 Sentence Smart

When we've saved enough money, we can buy an ox.

I want a large house but I need more coins.

p. 76 The Gift from the Giant

(Individual writing and drawing)

Story 5
Sally's Day at the Theme Park

p. 90 Do You Remember?

Before Meeting the Princess:
the Ghost Train

After Meeting the Princess:
the Big Dipper ; the Mermaid Ride ; the Carousel ; the Fairy Swings

p. 91 Missing Words

1. sunny
2. many
3. last
4. dark
5. (Suggested answer) scary
6. After
7. good

p. 92 Fun with Phonics

1. strawberries
2. Scrabble
3. screamed
4. splashed
5. strong
6. springtime
7. strong
8. springtime
9. strawberries
10. Scrabble
11. screamed ; splashed

p. 93 Sentence Smart

1. Are you having fun, Sally?
2. Wow! This is exciting, Mermaid!
3. "Sally, it is time to go home," Dad said.
4. "Was that just a dream or was it real?" thought Sally.

p. 94 Describe Them!

(Individual writing)

Story 6
Diamonds and Toads

p. 108 Do You Remember?

A. mother B. toads
C. sister D. pearls
C ; D ; B ; A

p. 109 Missing Words

1. rude ; selfish
2. caring ; gentle ; hard-working
3. greedy ; furious
4. just ; noble

p. 110 Fun with Phonics

Circle:
arrived ; well ; sitting ; Suddenly ; appearance ; actually ; lesson ; different ; fell
dd: suddenly
ff: different
ll: well ; actually ; fell
pp: appearance
rr: arrived
ss: lesson
tt: sitting

p. 111 Sentence Smart

1. They were always angry. ; A
2. The woman was a fairy. ; C
3. The rich woman was thirsty. ; D
4. The prince saw the jewels. ; B

p. 112 What Happened Next?

(Individual writing and drawing)

ISBN: 978-1-926884-05-9